A

SKILLS JOURNAL

¿Amazing English!™

AN INTEGRATED ESL CURRICULUM

Michael Walker

Addison-Wesley Publishing Company

A Publication of the World Language Division

Director of Product Development: Judith M. Bittinger
Executive Editor: Elinor Chamas
Content Development: Elly Schottman, Susan Hooper
Editorial Development: Elly Schottman
Text and Cover Design: Taurins Design Associates
Art Direction and Production: Taurins Design Associates
Production and Manufacturing: James W. Gibbons

Illustrators: Ellen Appleby 28, 38, 98; Lee Lee Brazeal 14, 22, 31, 51, 59, 78, 80, 93, 105; Mena Dolobowsky 5, 15, 16, 32 bottom, 45, 47, 60, 64, 67 top, 69, 73 top, 82 top, 100; Steve Henry 17, 25, 46, 52, 89, 92; Pat Hoggan 2, 13, 65, 66, 75, 76, 79, 81, 88; Gay Holland 85; Loretta Lustig 8, 83, 102; Susan Miller 1, 3, 4, 11, 21, 33, 44, 49, 94; Diane Paterson 63; Chris Reed 10, 24, 30, 43, 58, 61, 71, 87, 101, 107; John Sandford 57; Karen Schmidt 29, 34; Jerry Smath 6, 7, 12, 20, 32 top, 48, 56, 62, 67 bottom, 68, 73 bottom, 74, 82 top, 84; Jackie Snider 23, 27, 35, 36, 40, 50, 54, 96, 97; Sally Springer 9, 53, 77, 86, 106

ISBN 0-201-85344-2
4 5 6 7 8 9 10-CRS-99 98 97

CONTENTS

Me

My name is _____.

I am a ☐ ☐ girl.
            boy.

Draw your picture here.

© Addison-Wesley Publishing Company

(Supports Language Activities Big Book A, Activity 1) **Writing a personalized journal entry.** Students trace or write their first name, then put an X in the appropriate box, girl or boy. They draw a picture of themselves inside the frame. Students practice reading the completed page to partners and the teacher. You may want to save this page in the student's **Assessment Portfolio.**

(Activity Supports Language Activities Big Book A, Activity 2) **Tracking left to right; TPR.** Students point to the pictures (left to right; top to bottom) as they listen to the chant "Stand Up, Sit Down." Say chant together as students again point to pictures. Recite one line of the chant, have students point to the correct row. Ask students to mark a specific picture in that row. *Jump up, jump down, show me four. Good. Now point to "jump up."* Draw an X on the picture "jump up." Have students act out the TPR chant.

I

We can _____.

3

We can _____.

WORD BANK

jump

run

talk

(Supports Student Book A, page 3) **Home-School Connection.** Review Word Bank vocabulary at the bottom of pages 3-4. Sing and act out modified verses of the song using Word Bank words: *We can jump, we can jump, when we all go out to play.* Each student chooses three words to write on the lines, completing the sentences and illustrating each page. Provide help as needed. Cut out and staple take-home books together. Students practice reading completed book to partners and teacher. Save Word Bank strips in a safe place.

3

2

We can _____

4

when we all go out to play.

WORD BANK

climb

hop

sit

Draw your own playground.

WORD BANK

| swing | slide | tire | sandbox |

(Supports Student Book A, pages 4-6) **Drawing and labeling a map.** Students draw a "map" of a playground and label some of the equipment. The Word Bank strip will be cut out after students complete this theme. You may then want to save this page in the student's **Assessment Portfolio.**

WORD BANK

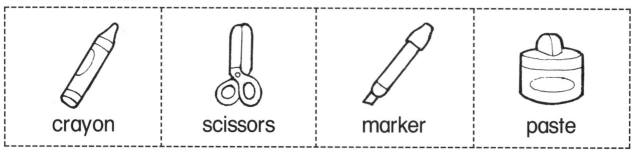

| crayon | scissors | marker | paste |

(Supports Language Activities Big Book A, Activity 3) **Figure-ground discrimination.** Students use small pictures as clues to find and circle hidden objects in big picture. Give directions for coloring hidden pictures: *Color the crayon red. Color the scissors yellow. Color the marker blue. Color the paste green.* The Word Bank strip will be cut out after students complete this theme.

6

1 one	
2 two	
3 three	
4 four	
5 five	

(Supports Big Book: *On the First Day of School*) **Counting; recognizing numerals; cooperative learning.**
Students draw a line from the numeral to the picture illustrating that number. Students then do pair work.
One partner points to a number box, the other says the number.

8

(Supports Language Activities Big Book A, Activity 4) **Counting; writing numerals.** For each picture, ask: *How many (girls) can you see?* Students answer, "(One)." They practice tracing the numerals. For additional practice, give coloring directions. *Point to the chairs. Color two chairs blue. Color two chairs red.*

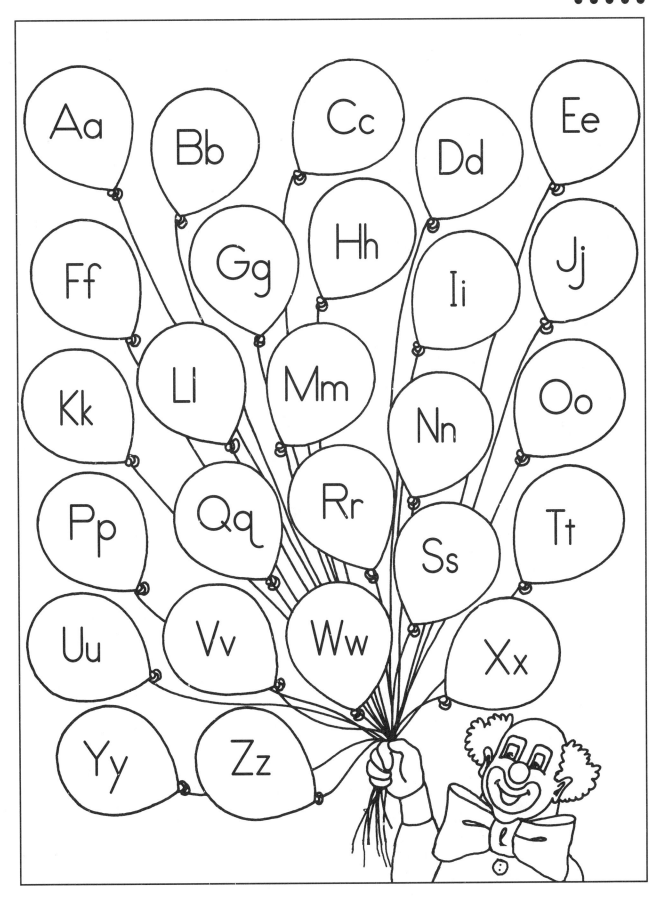

(Supports Student Book A, page 7) **Reciting, recognizing letters of alphabet.** Students point to the letters as they recite alphabet, or say the Alphabet Cheer, or sing the traditional alphabet song. Teacher then names a letter; students point to it, then color the balloon. A student or the teacher specifies what color to use.

Home-School Connection

Letter Pretzels

You need:

$1\frac{1}{2}$ cup warm water

1 package yeast

4 cups flour

1 tablespoon sugar

1 teaspoon salt

1. Put the water and the yeast in a bowl. Let it sit 5 minutes. Then stir.

2. Add the flour, sugar and salt. Mix well.

3. Roll the dough into long snake shapes.

4. Make the first letter of your name.

5. Cook in the oven.

EAT!

(Supports Student Book A, page 7) **Home-School Connection.** This recipe may be made in class and then sent home for family sharing. If you wish, you can brush the pretzels with beaten egg and sprinkle with coarse (kosher) salt.

Write about the kids you know.

Kids are _____ .

Kids are _____ .

Some kids have a
favorite buddy.

Me and My Buddy

WORD BANK

silly

funny

happy

muddy

(Supports Student Book A, pages 8-9) **Completing and personalizing a story.** Review and act out words in Word Bank. Students complete the sentences by writing two of these words on the lines. Students illustrate their story and read it to a partner and the teacher.

(Supports Student Book A, pages 8-9) **Initial letters and sounds.** Students name the objects on this page and identify the beginning sound and letter. They trace the letters: *Aa, Bb, Cc, Dd*. Give directions for coloring: *Find the picture that begins with a. Color it red. Find the pictures that begin with b. Color them blue. etc.*

My name is

_____
- -
_____ .

I can _____ .

I can _____ .

I can _____ .

WORD BANK

write	read	sing	draw

(Supports Language Activities Big Book A, Activity 5) **Writing a journal entry.** Review the Word Bank vocabulary. Students complete the first sentence by writing their first name. They complete the other sentences by
writing a word chosen from the Word Bank. Students read their stories to a partner and to the teacher. You
may want to save this page in the student's **Assessment Portfolio.**

Listen to the directions.

Draw a path.

Then talk about the map with a friend.

CAFETERIA

LIBRARY

SCHOOL

(Supports Language Activities Big Book A, Activity 6) **Practicing map skills.** Students use a pencil to trace a path through the school, following your directions. Read these directions. *Go into the school. Go into the office. Go out the other door. Go into room 1. Go into room 2. Go out of room 2. Now you're in the hall. Go into the library. Go into the cafeteria. Go out the other door. Now go out of the school. Get on the bus!*

Cut out the words at the bottom of the page.

Paste the words in the sentences.

Read the sentences.

This is a _____.

This is a _____.

This is a _____.

These are _____.

These are _____.

| monkey | backpack | erasers | ruler | pencils |

(Supports Big Book: *On the First Day of School*) **Matching words and pictures.** Read the sentence next to each picture together. Have students identify the object(s), then point to that word at the bottom of the page. Have students discuss their strategies for choosing the correct word. Have students cut out the word cards and glue them in the correct spots.

How many do you see?

monkeys _____

bears _____

rulers _____

scissors _____

16

(Supports Student Book A, pages 10-11) **Figure-ground discrimination; counting; writing numerals.** Read the question together. Students can work in pairs, finding and circling the hidden animals and objects. Students then count and write the numbers on the lines.

Spin and Draw

(Supports Student Book A, pages 12-13) **Following directions; recognizing numerals.** Students play the game "Spin and Draw" with a partner using the game board on Student Book page 13. At the end of each turn, they will add a certain number of objects to the classroom map on this page, following the game board directions.

Ask your friends:

"What's your name?"

Write the names here.

_____

- -

_____

_____

- -

_____

_____

- -

_____

_____

- -

_____

How many names are on your list? _____

Write your own name here.

_____

- -

_____

(Supports Student Book A, page 14) **Conducting a survey.** Each student asks several friends: *What's your name?* Either child can write the name on the line. Then, the student counts the names and writes the number. Confer briefly with each student, *Tell me about these names.* Jot down the student's responses. You may want to save this page in the student's **Assessment Portfolio.**

Cut the Word Bank cards from pages 3, 4, 5, 6, 11 and 13.
Choose nine cards to glue on this game board.
Then play a game of Amazing Words tic-tac-toe.

Key vocabulary reinforcement. Students prepare their game boards, then play a variation of tic-tac-toe with a partner. Each player has a different set of markers (paper clips, small pieces of colored paper, etc.) In order to place a marker on a square, a player must name the picture. The first player to place three markers in a row (horizontal, vertical, diagonal) wins the game. Save extra Word Bank cards for future use.

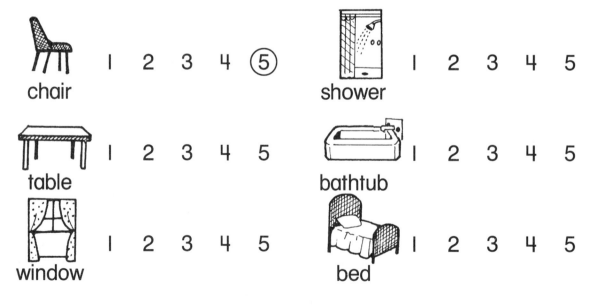

chair   1   2   3   4   ⑤

shower   1   2   3   4   5

table   1   2   3   4   5

bathtub   1   2   3   4   5

window   1   2   3   4   5

bed   1   2   3   4   5

20

(Supports Language Activities Big Book A, Activity 7) **Reinforcing vocabulary; counting; recognizing numerals.** Review the names of the objects at the bottom of the page. For each object, students count how many appear in the house diagram. They circle the correct number.

This is how to write **family** in Japanese. Trace the words. Draw a picture of your family.

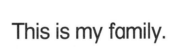

This is my family.

WORD BANK

mother

father

sister

brother

(Supports Student Book A, page 15) **Presenting information through drawings and labels.** Students trace the Japanese character for "family." Then they draw a portrait of their own family, and label the family members. The Word Bank provides some vocabulary and spelling assistance. You may wish to provide additional words for family members.

Finish the sentences. Write **in**, **on** or **under**.

The ☀ is _____ the 🪑 .

The 🐕 is _____ the 🛁 .

The 🐸 is _____ the 🪑 .

WORD BANK

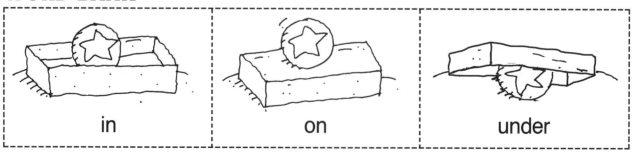

| in | on | under |

22 (Supports Language Activities Big Book A, Activity 8) **Completing sentences to match pictures.** Review the prepositions at the bottom of the page. Students look at the pictures and complete each sentence orally. They then write the correct prepositions on the lines, and read the sentences to a partner.

In My House

All day, I play.

All night, I sleep.

I like my house.

(Supports Student Book A, pages 16-18) **Building word recognition and analysis skills.** Read the story aloud together. Ask students: *What do you play all day? Where do you sleep at night?* Students personalize this story through their drawings. Use the page to build early reading skills. Have students track words as you read the first sentence aloud, then say, *Point to the word* I. *Can you see the word* I *somewhere else? Point to the word* day. *How do you spell* day? etc.

Breakfast with My Family

Set the table for your family.

Draw cups , napkins , plates , and bowls .

There is ☐ table.

There are ☐ cups.

There are ☐ plates.

WORD BANK

| cup | napkin | plate | bowl |

(Supports Language Activities Big Book A, Activity 9) **Counting; practicing language structure *There is/There are...*** Students "set the table" for their family by drawing plates, bowls, cups, and napkins on the table outline. Students complete sentences by counting and writing the number. Ask: *What's for breakfast?* Encourage diverse answers. You may want to save this page in the student's **Assessment Portfolio.**

Goodnight, _____
(Write a grown-up's name here.)

Goodnight, _____
(Write your name here.)

We say goodnight.
I go to bed.

(Supports Student Book A, pages 19-21) **Personalizing a story.** Ask: *Who do you say goodnight to?* Students personalize the drawing by completing the child as themselves; the adult outline becomes an adult to whom they say goodnight (mother, father, etc.) They write the name of their special adult in the speech bubble. They read their completed story to a partner and/or the teacher.

TORTILLAS

Tortillas, tortillas

Tortillas, for my mother,

Tortillas, tortillas,

Tortillas for my father,

Tortillas, tortillas

Tortillas for me!

(Supports Student Book A, page 22) **Home-School Connection.** Read the poem together. Use the text for building word analysis skills. *Find a word that begins with* (t, m, p). *Draw a line under the word* tortillas. *How many tortillas can you find? Point to a word you know. Read it.* Students illustrate the border of the poem, then take the page home to share with their family.

Ask your friends:

"How old are you?"

Write names here.

Color in the right number of candles.

(Supports Language Activities Big Book A, Activity 10) **Taking a survey, creating a graph.** Student writes own name on chart, and colors the box that shows his or her age. Then student asks several friends: *How old are you?* Either child can write the name on the line and color in the correct box. After the survey is finished, help students discuss and compare results.

Ee   Ff   Gg   Hh

_____at

_____inger

_____ar

_____oot

_____and

_____irl   _____randfather

(Supports Language Activities Big Book A, Activity 11) **Initial letters and sounds.** Trace the letters Ee, Ff, Gg, Hh. Name the two figures: *girl* and *grandfather*. Point out the words. Say, *The first letter is missing. What is the first letter in girl? In grandfather?* Have students write the missing *g*. Have students name the featured body parts and clothing, then identify and write the missing initial letters.

28

30

(Supports Big Book: *Goldilocks and the Three Bears*) **Following directions; recalling story events**. Stu
follow directions: *Draw a line under Baby Bear. Draw a circle around Papa Bear. Color Mama Bear's dre*
blue. Color Goldilocks' hair yellow. Then students cut out the four small pictures and place each charac
the appropriate chair or bed. Students describe each completed picture to partners and/or the teacher

Home-School Connection

Baby Bear's Porridge

You need:

$\frac{1}{4}$ cup instant oatmeal

$\frac{1}{2}$ cup milk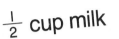

10 raisins

brown sugar

1. Stir the oatmeal, milk and raisins together.

2. Cook in the microwave or on a stove.

3. Add brown sugar.

This is just right!

EAT!

(Supports Big Book: *Goldilocks and the Three Bears*) **Home-School Connection.** If possible, bring ingredients to class and do this cooking project with your students before sending the recipe home.

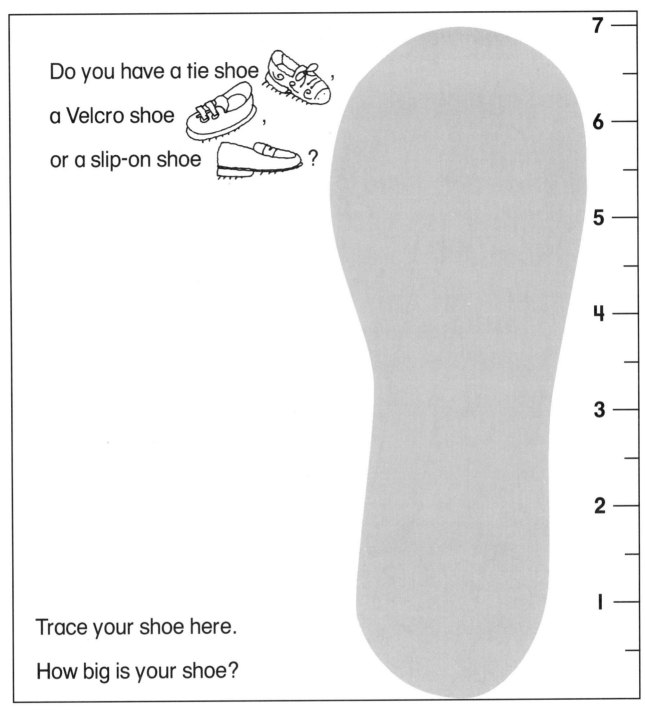

Do you have a tie shoe ,

a Velcro shoe ,

or a slip-on shoe ?

7

6

5

4

3

2

1

Trace your shoe here.

How big is your shoe?

(Supports Student Book A, page 23) **Classifying, measuring, cooperative learning.** Read the question at the top of the page together. Have students circle the answer. Demonstrate how students can work in pairs and trace each other's shoe. The heel must be on the base line. Students circle the number on the ruler that is the closest measurement. Circulate as students work. Ask, *How big is your shoe?* ("Six inches.")

WORD BANK

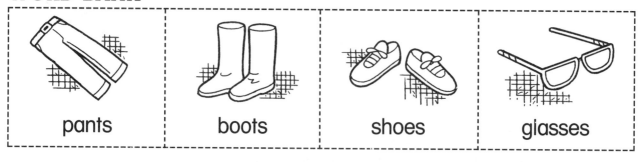

pants   boots   shoes   glasses

32 (Supports Language Activities Big Book A, Activity 12) **Describing clothes; cooperative learning.** Students color the man and woman's clothes as they wish. Then they work with a partner and ask each other questions: *What color are his (shoes)?*

Draw a picture of yourself.
What are you doing?

I am _____ .

WORD BANK

| writing | drawing | painting | talking |

(Supports Language Activities Big Book A, Activity 13) **Writing a sentence.** Students draw themselves doing
an activity, then complete the sentence below the picture. Students may use a verb illustrated in the Word
Bank or choose a different activity. Students may use invented (approximated) spelling or standard spelling.
With some students, you may want to use a collaborative writing technique. You may want to save this page
in the student's **Assessment Portfolio.**

She ran all the way home.

This chair is too hard.

This bed is just right.

This porridge is just right.

(Supports Big Book: *Goldilocks and the Three Bears*) **Sequencing; retelling the story.** Discuss the pictures with the students. Ask volunteers to read the sentences aloud or read them together. Students write the numbers 1, 2, 3, and 4 to show the proper sequence of the pictures. Have students practice in pairs, reading the sentences and retelling the story.

(Supports Student Book A, page 26) **Constructing a "family tree."** Students draw pictures of family members in these frames. They cut out the frames and write the name of the person on the back. These pictures can be hung from a "family tree" branch, as shown on Student Book page 26. Talk about the shapes and sizes of the frames and the pictures drawn by the students: *Show me the (big, little) (circle, square). Who is that?*

35

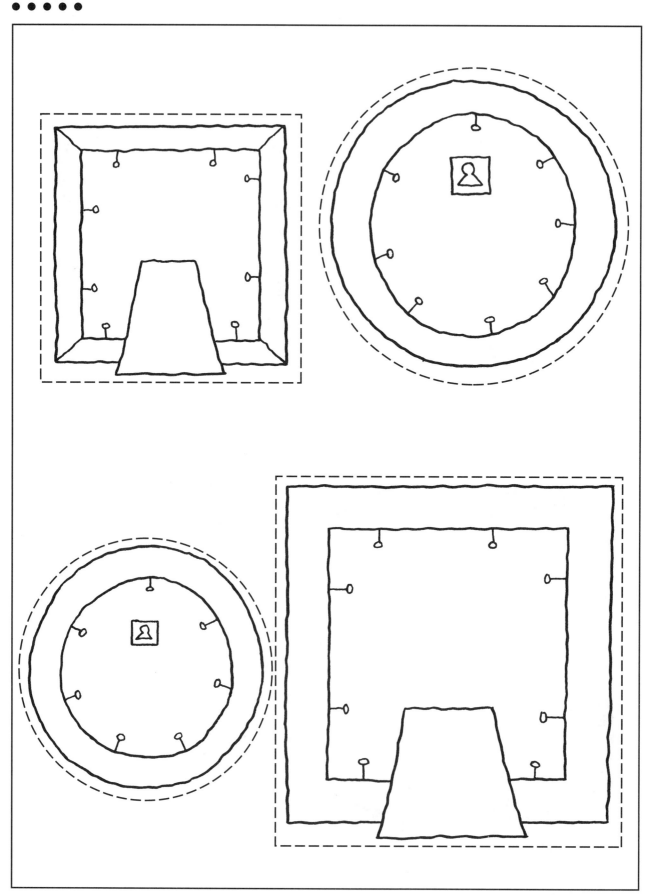

Cut the Word Banks cards from pages 21, 22, 32, and 33.

Choose nine cards to glue on this game board.

Then play a game of Amazing Words tic-tac-toe.

Key vocabulary reinforcement. Students prepare their game boards, then play a variation of tic-tac-toe with a partner. Each player has a different set of markers (paper clips, small pieces of colored paper, etc.) In order to place a marker on a square, a player must name the picture. The first player to place three markers in a row (horizontal, vertical, diagonal) wins the game. Save extra Word Bank cards for future use.

MORE ABOUT ME

At Home

At School

I _____ at home.

(Supports Language Activities Big Book A, Activity 14) **Classifying.** Students circle the pictures in each column that match the heading, "At Home" or "At School." Then they talk about the pictures: *Where is s/he? At home or at school? What is s/he doing? What do you do at home?* Students complete the sentence at the bottom of the page using invented (approximated) spelling.

38

Ask your friends:

"What's your phone number?"

Name_____

Phone Number _____

• •

Name_____

Phone Number _____

• •

Name_____

Phone Number _____

• •

Name_____

Phone Number _____

• •

(Supports Language Activities Big Book A, Activity 15) **Conducting a survey, analyzing data.** Student asks several friends: *What's your phone number?* Either child can write the name and phone number on the chart. After the survey is finished, help students discuss and compare the data: *How are the phone numbers alike?*

Sometimes I think about

_____

- -

_____.

(Supports Student Book A, page 27) **Writing a journal entry.** Ask, *Do you sometimes like to be alone? What do you think about when you're alone?* After a brief brainstorming discussion, have each student draw something he or she thinks about, then complete the sentence below the picture. You may want to save this page in the student's **Assessment Portfolio.**

Home-School Connection

I Like You.

We live together
happily.

⑦

You have_____

_____.

⑤

I play_____

_____.

②

(Supports Big Book: *I Like You*) **Home-School Connection; cooperative learning.** Help students cut, fold,
and assemble this take-home book on pages 41 and 42. Staple the spine together. Read the book.
Demonstrate how students will work in pairs to complete their books, asking each other, *What do you have?*
What do you eat? Students illustrate each page and complete the sentences. Provide help as needed.

by

_____

_ _ _ _ _ _ _ _ _ _ _ _ _

_____

(your name)

and

_____

_ _ _ _ _ _ _ _ _ _ _ _ _

_____

(buddy's name)

①

I like you.

You like me.

⑥

You play_____

_____.

③

I have_____

_____.

④

Home-School Connection

Tiger Paws

You need:

refrigerator biscuits

slivered almonds

sugar

cinnamon

1. Cut each biscuit into three pieces.

2. Shape each piece to be short and fat.

3. Push the pieces together to make a "paw."

4. Push three almond "claws" into the "paw."

5. Sprinkle with sugar and cinnamon.

6. Bake in the oven.

EAT!

(Supports Student Book A, pages 28-31) **Home-School Connection.** If possible bring ingredients to class and do this cooking project with your students before sending the recipe home.

Today, Today, Today

What are you going to do today?
I'm going to ride my bike today.
What are you going to do today?
I'm going to ride my bike today.

She's going to ride her bike today,
Today, today, today, today.
She's going to ride her bike today,
Today, today, today, today.

Draw your own picture.
Sing your own verse.

I'm going to _____ today.

44

(Supports Student Book A, page 32) **Building word recognition skills.** Students point to each word as they listen to the song verse. Then they sing the verse. Ask questions about the print. (You may want to make an overhead transparency of this page.) *Show me the title. Read it. Can you find the word* today *somewhere else on this page? Who can find the word* bike? *How many times can you find the word* bike? Brainstorm ideas for new verses, then have students complete the bottom of the page.

(Supports Language Activities Big Book A, Activity 16) **Classifying.** Point to each picture on this page and ask: *What is (he, she, it) doing?* Then have students draw a line connecting the two pictures that show the same action. One example is done. Have students check and discuss their work with a partner.

45

1. _____

2. _____

3. _____

4. _____

WORD BANK

 firefighter |  police officer |  letter carrier |  bus driver

(Supports Language Activities Big Book A, Activity 17) **Labeling pictures.** Review the Word Bank vocabulary and discuss the main illustration. Ask: *Where is the (fire fighter)? Who is in the (bus)? Show me the police officer. Find number 4. Who is it?* etc. Have students write the name of the workers on the lines.

Cut out the pictures.
Find the pictures that go together.
Finish the sentences by pasting the pictures in the box.

I see a [ ].

It's part of a [ ].

· ·

I see a [ ].

It's part of a [ ].

· ·

I see a [ ].

It's part of a [ ].

 zipper
 bow
 button
 shirt
 jacket
 shoe

(Supports Student Book A, page 33-34) **Recognizing parts of a whole.** Review the names of the pictures at the bottom of the page. Read the incomplete sentence pairs together. Discuss which pairs of pictures could correctly complete these sentences. Have students cut and paste the pictures, then read the completed sentences to a partner.

47

Ii   Jj   Kk   Ll

1. __acket

2. __unchbox

3. __itchen

4. __ce cream

(Supports Student Book A, page 33-34) **Initial letters and sounds.** Students trace *Ii, Jj, Kk, Ll* at the top of the page. Ask, *Does anyone's name begin with I, J, K, or L? What sound does that letter make at the beginning of your name?* Together, name the four objects on this page and identify the beginning sound and letter. Have students write the missing initial letter on the line.

My Feelings

I'm _____.

I'm _____.

WORD BANK

| happy | mad | sad | hungry | tired |

(Supports Student Book A, page 35) **Writing a journal entry.** Review and mime the words in the Word Bank. Say, *If you're (hungry), raise your hand.* Have students write words of their choice to complete the sentences, then illustrate their sentences. Confer with students, *Read your sentence. Tell me about your picture.* You may want to save this page in the student's **Assessment Portfolio.**

Draw an X on the picture that does not belong.

Games	Pets
basketball	cat
dog	jump rope
soccer	iguana
hopscotch	bird
Draw a game.	Draw a pet.

(Supports Big Book: *I Like You*) **Classifying.** Read the words in each column together. Students place an X on the picture in each column that does not belong. Students then draw a game of their choice at the bottom of the *Games* column and a pet of their choice at the bottom of the *Pets* column. Encourage students to write the name of their game and pet.

50

What's wrong?

What did he hurt?
Write the word on the line.

WORD BANK

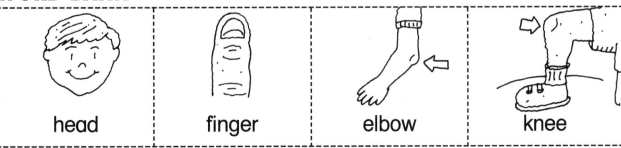

| head | finger | elbow | knee |

(Supports Language Activities Big Book A, Activity 18) **Labeling a diagram.** Review the Word Box vocabulary.
Have a student volunteer clutch his or her head, finger, elbow, or knee as you ask the class, *What did (he)*
hurt? The class will reply, *He hurt his (knee).* Have students label the diagram on this page, then point to a
word and practice the dialog with a partner.

I'm going to

_____

the _____ ,

I'm going to

feed the elephant.

I'm going to

_____

the _____ .

I'm going to play

on the swings.

WORD BANK

supermarket   park   zoo   restaurant

(Supports Language Activities Big Book A, Activity 19) **Drawing conclusions.** Review the Word Box vocabulary. Draw attention to each picture scene and ask, *Where is (she)?* Read the accompanying sentences aloud with the class, allowing students to supply the missing word. Students will then write the words on the correct lines, and practice reading the sentences with a partner. Students can suggest their own sentences for the remaining two pictures, *supermarket* and *restaurant*.

Mm Nn Oo Pp

Make a ___icture of a monster.

The ___onster has a big ___ose.

He's wearing ___veralls.

(Supports Language Activities Big Book A, Activity 19) **Initial letters and sounds.** Students trace the letters at the top of the page. Ask, *Does anyone's name begin with M, N, O, or P? What sound does that letter make at the beginning of your name?* Read the story together, letting students supply the pictured words when possible. Review the names of the four pictures. Students identify the beginning sound and letter, write the letter on the line, and read the completed story to each other.

Draw a shape dog.
Then count the shapes, and fill in the chart.

Girl   Dog

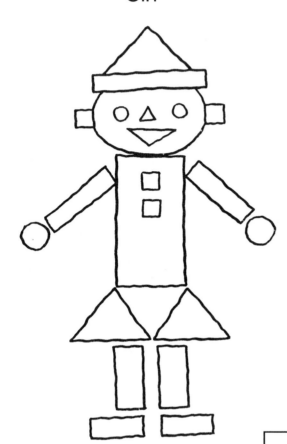

How many circles ⬡ ?

How many rectangles ▭?

How many triangles △ ?

How many squares ☐?

	Girl	Dog

(Supports Student Book A, pages 38) **Identifying shapes; counting.** Have students identify the four shapes used to make the Girl on this page: *circle, rectangle, triangle, square.* Students will use the same four shapes to make a Dog. (Students may draw or use paper shapes that you provide.) As a class, count the number of circles, rectangles, etc. in the Girl and write the numbers in the chart. Have students work in pairs, counting the shapes in their Dogs and filling in the chart.

Cut the Word Bank cards from pages 46, 48, 51, and 52.

Choose nine cards to glue on this game board.

Then play a game of Amazing Words tic-tac-toe.

Key vocabulary reinforcement. Students prepare their game boards, then play a variation of tic-tac-toe with a partner. Each player has a different set of markers (paper clips, small pieces of colored paper, etc.) In order to place a marker on a square, a player must name the picture. The first player to place three markers in a row (horizontal, vertical, diagonal) wins the game. Save extra Word Bank cards for future use.

EVERYBODY EATS!

I like to   I don't like to

1.
2.
3.
4.
5.
6.

(Supports Language Activities Big Book A, Activity 20) **Expressing likes and dislikes.** Discuss each picture.
Ask students, *Do you like to (wash dishes)? Yes, I do./ No, I don't.* Students draw a happy face or a sad face
depending on their response. Students draw a picture of an activity they like to do next to the happy face at
the bottom of the page. They talk about their picture to a partner and/or the teacher.

Take the Gingerbread Man through the maze.
Tell the story to a friend.

START HERE

THE END!

(Supports Big Book: *The Gingerbread Man*) **Solving a maze, sequencing, retelling a story.** As students trace a path through the maze, they pass through three scenes from the story of *The Gingerbread Man*. They use the completed maze as a story map as they retell the story of *The Gingerbread Man* to a partner.

57

Make your own verse.
What is on your plate?

_____ on my plate.

_____ on my plate.

_____ it up. _____ it up.

_____ on my plate.

WORD BANK

spaghetti

soup

ice cream

cookie

cereal

(Supports Student Book A, pages 39) **Creating original poem verses.** As a class, create several new verses to the poem "Spaghetti on My Plate," using the food words in the Word Bank. Each student then chooses how to complete his or her own verse and illustrates the verse. (Example: *Ice cream on my plate. Ice cream on my plate. Lick it up. Lick it up. Ice cream on my plate.*)

58

What will you buy?

Circle a food that begins with each letter on the shopping list.
Write the words on the shopping list.

Shopping List

b

c

m

j

p

(Supports Student Book A, pages 40-41) **Applying knowledge of letters and sounds.** Review the names of the foods, then draw attention to the shopping list. Ask: *Which foods begin with the letter (p)?* Students write the (p) word of their choice (*peas* or *potatoes*) on the list. Encourage students to use their knowledge of letters and sound to do "best guess" spelling. Students read their completed list to a partner. You may want to save this page in the student's **Assessment Portfolio.**

Home-School
Connection

I Like Pizza

I like _____,

You like _____.

We like jumping very high.

I like _____,

You like_____.

Of all my friends, I like you most.

© Addison-Wesley Publishing Company

WORD BANK

pizza

pie

tacos

toast

(Supports Student Book A, pages 42-43) **Home-School Connection.** Review the Word Bank vocabulary. Students complete the poem by writing the correct word on each line. Have students cut off the Word Bank strip and save it for later classroom use. Students practice reading the poem aloud to a partner and then take the poem home to share with their families.

Draw your favorite foods.
Write the words on the lines.

Foods I Like

(Supports Language Activities Big Book A, Activity 21) **Writing a journal entry.** Have a class discussion about favorite foods. You may want to make a list of foods students mention. Have students complete their journal entry by drawing and writing the names of the five foods they like best.

"Run, run, run,
As fast as you can.
You can't catch me,
I'm the   ."

(Supports Big Book, *The Gingerbread Man*) **Identifying story characters, discussing sentence capitalization and punctuation.** Students find and color the hidden characters from the story. They read the refrain of the story, pointing to the words. Check understanding of print and discuss print conventions (capitalization, punctuation, quotation marks): *Show me a word you know. Read it. Find the word,* run. *How many times can you find the word* run? *Why does this* Run *start with a capital R?*

I want

  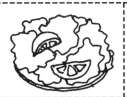 

(Supports Language Activities Big Book A, Activity 22) **Creating dialogue for a restaurant role-play.** Review names of the food items at the bottom of the page. Students cut out food items and choose two to paste into each thought balloon. They work in groups of three, role-playing the restaurant scene. Students draw the food they'd like to order in the box. They "read" their order to a partner and/or the teacher.

63

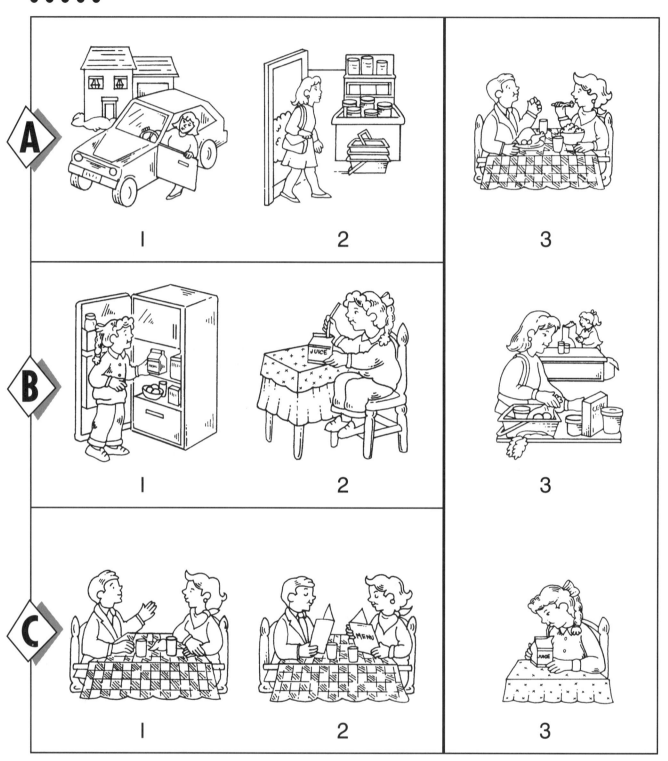

(Supports Language Activities Big Book A, Activity 23) **Drawing conclusions.** Discuss the actions taking place in scenes 1 and 2, shown in each row. Have students decide which picture completes each sequence, and draw a line from the row to the correct picture.

A take-home book to share
with your family.
⑦

Two Greedy Bears
A folktale from Eastern Europe

Now Magda has
more than me.

OK. I'll take a bite
from Magda's
cheese.

⑤

Give it to me!

No. Give it to me.

②

Supports Student Book A, pages 44-48) **Home-School Connection.** Help students cut, fold, and assemble
this take-home book. Staple the spine together. Students may want to color the pictures. Have students work
in pairs, reading and role-playing the dialogue. Students will take the book home to share with their families.

Food	Sweet	Sour	Salty
a lemon			
an orange			
a potato chip			

I like _____ food.

(Supports Language Activities Big Book A, Activity 24) **Classifying, recording data on a chart.** Provide lemon and orange slices and potato chips. If possible, bring at least one other sweet, sour, and salty food (Examples: jelly, pickle, pretzel). Students taste lemon, orange and potato chips, decide if each is sweet, sour, or salty, and mark the correct column. Students taste the other food and enter the information on the chart. Students complete the sentence at the bottom of the page and illustrate it.

67

Qq Rr Ss Tt

1. ____adio

2. ____ocks

3. ____able

4. ____andals

5. ____urtle

6. ____ueen

(Supports Language Activities Big Book A, Activity 25) **Initial letters and sounds.** Students trace the letters at the top of the page. Ask, *Does anyone's name begin with Q, R, S, or T? What sound does that letter make at the beginning of your name?* Together, name the objects on this page and identify the beginning sound and letter. Have students write the missing initial letter on the line.

_____

- - - - - - - - - - - - - - - - - - - 's Sandwich

(Write your name here)

What's in your sandwich?
Draw and write.

My sandwich has _____

_____

in it.

WORD BANK

lettuce

tomato

cheese

peanut
butter

jelly

(Supports Student Book A, pages 49) **Writing a journal entry.** Review the Word Bank vocabulary. Ask students: _What do you like in your sandwich?_ Encourage lots of different responses. Students write their names at the top of the page, draw the filling for their sandwich, then complete the sentence at the bottom of the page. Ask students to read their sentences aloud. You may want to save this page in the student's **Assessment Portfolio.**

Ask your friends:

"What do you eat in the morning?"

Draw.   Draw.   Draw.

How many kids   How many kids   How many kids
eat this? _____   eat this? _____   eat this? _____

What is the favorite morning food?

_____

_____

_____

(Supports Student Book A, pages 50-51) **Taking a survey; recording data.** Ask students: *What do you eat in the morning?* List their responses. Have the class choose three of these foods to use in this survey. Have them draw these foods in the boxes at the top of the page. Before students begin their surveys, demonstrate how to record a person's answer by filling in a box below the correct picture. After the survey, students answer the question at the bottom of the page. Help students discuss and compare their results.

Home-School Connection

Salsa Recipe

You need:

I can whole tomatoes

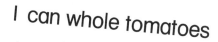

$\frac{1}{4}$ cup chopped onion

$\frac{1}{2}$ teaspoon vinegar

I tablespoon oil

I teaspoon oregano

I teaspoon chopped parsley

1. Crush the tomatoes. Put them in a bowl.

2. Add the rest of the ingredients.

3. Stir well.

4. Eat with taco chips!

(Supports Student Book A, page 52) **Home-School Connection.** If possible, bring ingredients to class and do this cooking project with your students before sending the recipe home.

71

Cut the Word Bank cards from pages 58, 60 and 69.

Choose nine cards to glue on this game board.

Then play a game of Amazing Words tic-tac-toe.

Key vocabulary reinforcement. Students prepare their game boards, then play a variation of tic-tac-toe with a partner. Each player has a different set of markers (paper clips, small pieces of colored paper, etc.) In order to place a marker on a square, a player must name the picture. The first player to place three markers in a row (horizontal, vertical, diagonal) wins the game. Save extra Word Bank cards for future use.

Farmer Brown's Day

He _____ .

He _____ .

He _____ .

(Supports Language Activities Big Book A, Activity 26.) **Creating and reading a rebus story.** Students study the pictures at the bottom of the page and describe what Farmer Brown does every day. They cut out the pictures and paste them in the story in the order they wish. Then they read their rebus story to a partner or teacher.

73

(Supports Student Book A, page 53) **Classifying.** Students work in pairs to find the picture in each row that does not belong with the others. They mark their choice with an X. Students explain the reasons for their choices in a class discussion.

Write the name of each animal.
Then write what it says.

WORD BANK

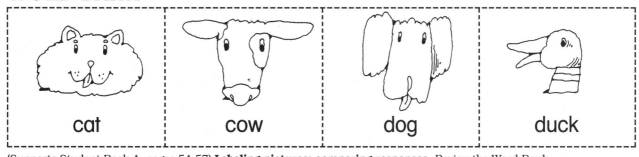

| cat | cow | dog | duck |

(Supports Student Book A, pages 54-57) **Labeling pictures; comparing responses**. Review the Word Bank
vocabulary. Students write the correct word below each animal picture. Ask: *What does a (dog) say?*
Encourage lots of different responses. Students write a sound each animal makes in the speech bubble. They
may use words used in their native language, an invented sound, or an English language sound. Classmates
share their work.

Ask your friends:

"What's your favorite animal?"

Color a footprint next to that animal.

pony						
rooster						
cow						
rabbit						

What's your favorite animal? _____

What animal do most of your friends like best?

_____

_____

_____

(Supports Language Activities Big Book A, Activity 27) **Taking a survey, creating a graph.** Students conduct a survey and create a picture bar graph of the results. After the survey is completed, students answer the questions at the bottom of the page. Classmates compare and discuss their survey results. You may want to save this page in the student's **Assessment Portfolio.**

Uu Vv Ww Xx Yy Zz

1. _____est

2. _____mbrella

3. _____atch

4. _____oo

(Supports Language Activities Big Book A, Activity 27) **Initial letters and sounds.** Students trace the letters at the top of the page. Ask, *does anyone's name begin with U, V, W, X, Y, or Z? What sound does that letter make at the beginning of your name?* Together, name the objects on this page and identify the beginning sound and letter. Have students write the missing initial letter on the line.

WORD BANK

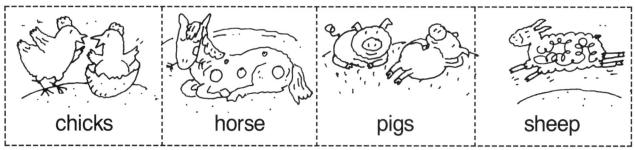

| chicks | horse | pigs | sheep |

(Supports Student Book A, page 58) **Labeling pictures, following directions**. Review the Word Bank vocabulary. Students write the correct word by each animal picture. Give drawing and coloring directions: *Draw four flowers. Color one chick yellow.* Encourage students to give similar drawing and coloring directions to the class.

Who does the Very Fine Rooster talk to first?
Who does he talk to next?
Draw a line along the road to show where the
Rooster goes.

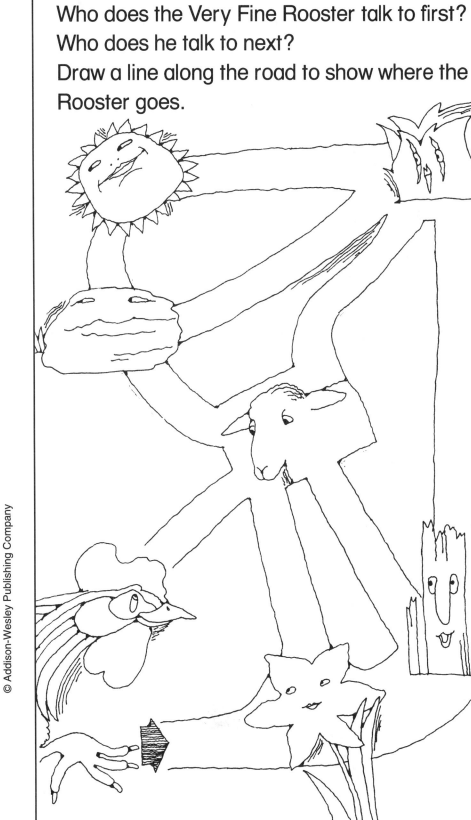

(Supports Big Book: *The Very Fine Rooster*) **Sequencing, retelling a story.** Students recall the story of *The Very Fine Rooster* as you ask: *Who did the rooster talk to first? Who did he talk to next?* As they answer each question, they draw a line along the road to show the rooster's route. Then they use their map to retell the story to a partner, the teacher, and/or their family.

Three Little Monkeys

[   ] little monkeys

Jumping on the [   ].

[   ] fell off

And bumped his [   ].

[   ] called the doctor

And the [   ] said,

"No more [   ]

[   ] on the bed!"

(Supports Student Book A, page 59) **Home-School Connection.** Recite the poem "Three Little Monkeys" together, as students point to the words on the page. Working with a partner, students cut out and paste the rebus pictures in the correct spaces. Check for correctness, then have students take home this rebus poem to share with their families.

Read each sentence.
Draw a line to the correct picture.

There are nine turtles.

There are six fish.

There are eight frogs.

There are seven birds.

(Supports Language Activities Big Book A, Activity 28) **Matching pictures and sentences.** Students work in pairs, reading the sentences and drawing a line to the correct picture.

81

WORD BANK

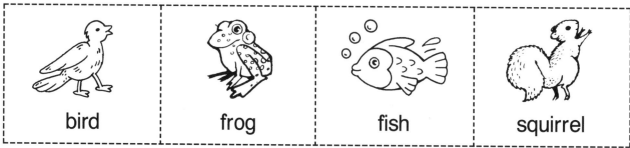

| bird | frog | fish | squirrel |

(Supports Language Activities Big Book A, Activity 29) **Describing location.** Review Word Bank vocabulary.
Students cut out pictures at the bottom of the page and paste them in appropriate place in the big scene.
They then describe the location of the animals to a partner and/or the teacher: *This (fish) is (in the water).*
This (frog) is (on the rock).

children

shovel

1. ___air

2. ___irt

3. ___oes

4. ___alkboard

(Supports Language Activities Big Book A, Activity 30) **Initial digraphs *ch* and *sh*.** Help students pronounce the words *children* and *shovel*, emphasizing the difference between the *ch* and *sh* sounds. Students trace the initial letters to complete the sample words. Then they name the remaining pictures and write the initial sounds. Partners then take turns reading the words to each other.

83

Farmer Brown **Farmer Red**

(Supports Language Activities Big Book A, Activity 31) **Obtaining information from illustrations.** Introduce the men in the pictures as Farmer Brown and Farmer Red. Ask: *What does Farmer Brown have? What does Farmer Red have?* Students color the YES or NO box in the charts below to show what each farmer has and doesn't have. Then they take turns naming one item that each farmer has and doesn't have.

How Do Owls Grow?

| 1 | 2 | 3 |

Draw a picture. Show how barn owls take good care of their babies.

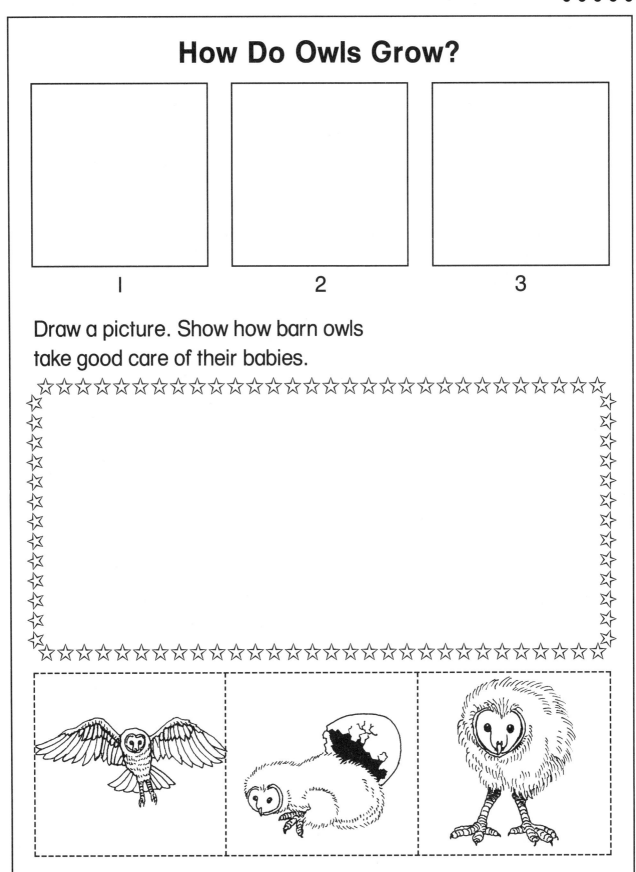

(Supports Student Book A, pages 60-61) **Sequencing; applying information.** Students examine the pictures at the bottom of the page and describe what is happening in each. They cut out the pictures and paste them in the proper sequence at the top of the page. They think about the facts they have learned and draw a picture and write a sentence to show how barn owls take care of their babies.

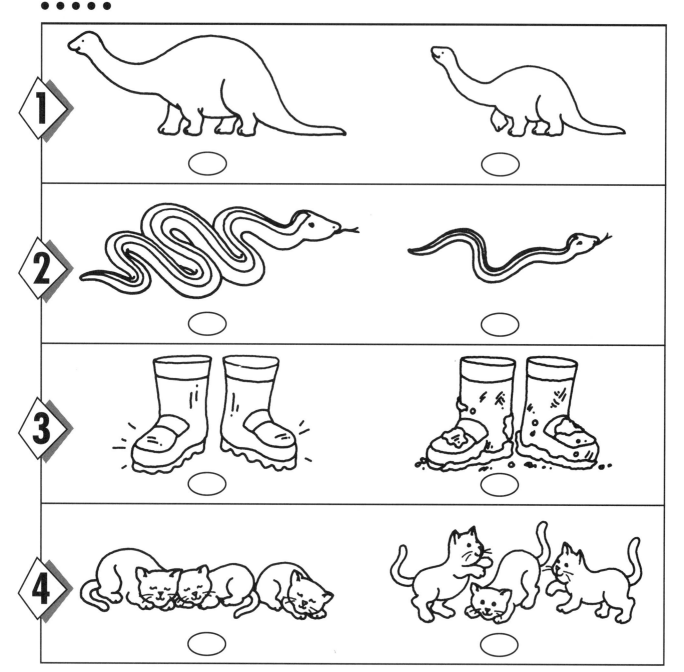

(Supports Language Activities Big Book A, Activity 32) **Preparation for standardized testing.** Students fill in the oval below the picture that matches the following description. *Row 1: This one is smaller. Row 2: This snake is longer. Row 3: These boots are dirty. Row 4: Those kittens are asleep.*

Home-School Connection

Chicken Feed for Kids

You need:

2 cups oats cereal

1 cup peanuts

$\frac{1}{2}$ cup sunflower seeds

$\frac{1}{2}$ cup raisins

1 cup chocolate bits

1. Mix in a bowl.

2. Serve in paper cups.

This is a great snack to take on a hike!

(Supports Big Book: *The Very Fine Rooster*) **Home-School Connection.** If possible, bring ingredients to school so students can make this recipe in class. Then send the recipe home for students to enjoy with their families.

I'll dry up the water.

But you have to do something for me.

You have to wake me up every morning.

The next morning…

| Kikiriki! | OK, I promise. | Good morning, rooster! |

(Supports Big Book: *The Very Fine Rooster*) **Recalling story events.** Discuss the top picture scene. Ask, *What do you think the rooster says?* Encourage students to retell the story using the picture strip in the middle of the page. Discuss the bottom scene. Have volunteers read the words at the bottom of the page. Students cut out the dialogue strips and glue them in the appropriate speech bubble.

(Supports Student Book A, page 64) **Classifying.** Give each child a large sheet of paper with five 3" wide columns. On the top of the five columns, students should write: *hop, swim, walk, fly, wiggle.* Students cut out the pictures on this page and place each animal in an appropriate column. Then they compare and discuss charts. There are often several correct placements for an animal.

Cut the Word Bank cards from pages 75, 78, and 82.
Choose nine cards to glue on this game board.
Then play a game of Amazing Words tic-tac-toe.

Key vocabulary reinforcement. Students prepare their game boards, then play a variation of tic-tac-toe with a partner. Each player has a different set of markers (paper clips, small pieces of colored paper, etc.) In order to place a marker on a square, a player must name the picture. The first player to place three markers in a row (horizontal, vertical, diagonal) wins the game. Save extra Word Bank cards for future use.

OUTSIDE MY WINDOW

Where is the bus  going?

Where is the car going?

Where is the truck going?

Follow the lines and find out.

BANK

FOOD

(Supports Language Activities Big Book A, Activity 33) **Following a maze.** Read the directions together. Name the vehicles and the places shown at the ends of the tangled roads. Students use first a finger, then three crayons of different colors to trace each tangled road and find where each vehicle is going.

I'm glad the sky is painted blue,

And the earth is painted green

With such a lot of nice fresh air

All sandwiched in between.

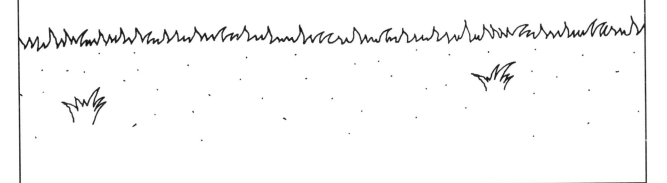

(Supports Student Book A, page 65) **Home-School Connection.** Practice reading the poem together. Have students follow directions to add animals and objects to the border art. *Draw a tree. Draw a rabbit under the tree. Draw a bird in the sky. Color the bird red. Color the rabbit brown. Color the sky blue. Color the grass green.* Students practice reading the poem to each other before taking it home to share with their families.

Look at pages 66-67 in the Student Book.

Do you spy a butterfly  ?
Where is it?

_____

- -

_____

List three other things hidden in the picture.
Ask a friend to find them.

I spy _____

- ,

and _____

- ,

and _____

- .

(Supports Student Book A, pages 66-67) **Identifying and describing hidden pictures; cooperative learning.**
Students search the photo scene on pages 66-67 for additional objects and write their findings on this page.
They prepare an original "I Spy" search for a partner.

Ask your friends:

"What can you do?"

Each friend can write his or her name in just one box.
Try to get a name in every box.

I can whistle.	I can snap my fingers.
I can spell my name backwards.	I can touch my tongue to my nose.
I can touch my foot to my head.	I can say "hello" in three languages.

(Supports Language Activities Big Book A, Activity 34) **Taking a survey; analyzing the data.** Read and discuss the sentences and the directions for conducting the survey. After the survey is completed, have students compare and discuss their findings.

Draw pictures for the story, "See for Yourself."
Tell the story to a friend.

(Supports Student Book A, pages 68-71) **Recalling story events, creating a story map**. As a class, discuss five pictures you could draw to retell the story "See for Yourself." Have students draw the illustrations, then use this story map to retell the folktale to a partner, the teacher, and/or their family.

Write a list poem about winter.
Draw a picture to go with your poem.

Winter

(Supports Language Activities Big Book A, Activity 35) **Writing an original poem.** Have students brainstorm a list of winter things. Ask, *What do you see in winter? What do you do in winter? Name some things you like about winter. Name some things you don't like about winter.* Write the children's ideas on a chart. Each child then writes his or her own list poem about winter.

S	M	T	W	T	F	S
1	2	3	4	5	6	7
8	9	10	11	12	13	14
15	16	17	18	19	20	21
22	23	24	25	26	27	28
29	30	31				

_____ ⬜ How many?

_____ ⬜ How many?

_____ ⬜ How many?

WORD BANK

 sunny    cloudy   rainy    windy    snowy

(Supports Language Activities Big Book A, Activity 36) **Using a calendar.** Review Word Bank vocabulary. Have students point to the numbers on the calendar as you count up to 31 in chorus. Students count the number of sunny, rainy, and windy days during the month. They write the name of the symbol on the line and the number in the box. As a follow-up, have students count and record the numbers of cloudy and snowy days.

big

bigger

biggest

fast

faster

fastest

(Supports Big Book: *The Most Wonderful One of All*) **Sequencing.** Ask three tall students to stand up. Ask: *Who is biggest?* Model the sentences: *(Joe) is big. (Mona) is bigger. (Luis) is biggest.* Ask students to name three fast animals. Draw sketches and/or write the names on pieces of paper. Have students sequence the animals in order of speed. Model the comparative sentences. Brainstorm other big and fast things for students to draw: animals, vehicles, buildings, etc. Have students work in pairs to complete the page.

What season is it? Write the word.
Then circle the clothes you would wear.

It's _____
        _____ .

It's _____
        _____ .

It's _____
        _____ .

WORD BANK

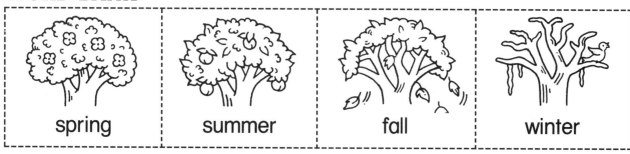

| spring | summer | fall | winter |

(Supports Language Activities Big Book A, Activity 37) **Classifying.** Review the Word Bank vocabulary. Have students write the name of the correct season on each line, then circle the appropriate clothing.

Draw a garden. What is growing in your garden?
Write the words next to your pictures.

What do the plants need to grow?

_____

- -

_____

- -

_____

WORD BANK

 flowers

 lettuce

 beans

 tomatoes

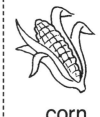 corn

(Supports Student Book A, page 72-74) **Drawing and labeling a diagram**. Review the words in the Word Bank
and read the directions together. Students can use the Word Bank to help label their garden diagram.
Students can refer to the article "City Gardens" to answer the final question. Encourage students to share and
discuss their work. You may want to save this page in the student's **Assessment Portfolio.**

101

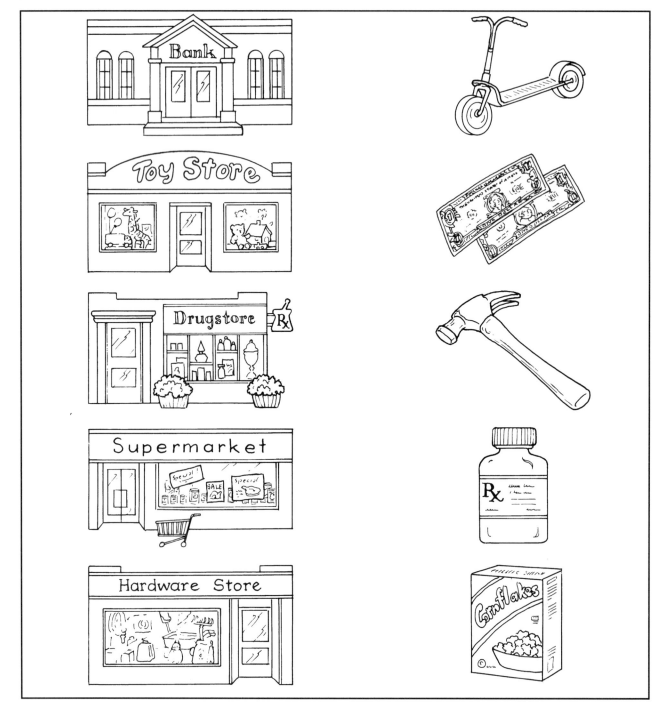

(Supports Language Activities Big Book A, Activity 38) **Classifying.** Students draw lines from each building to the item one can buy or get in that building. Then students ask each other questions: *Where can I get a (hammer)? At the (hardware store).*

The mothers on the bus go,
"Sh, sh, sh!"

The wheels on the bus go
round and round.

The driver on the bus goes,
"Move on back."
⑥

The horn on the bus goes
honk, honk, honk.

(Supports Student Book A, page 75) **Home-School Connection.** Students cut out, assemble, and staple their books. Then they read or sing the verses together and illustrate each page. They take their books home to share with their families.

The babies on the bus go
"Waa, waa waa."
②

The wipers on the bus go
swish, swish, swish.
⑦

The people on the bus go up
and down.
④

The money on the bus goes
clink, clink, clink.
⑤

Build a Wall

How to play:

Throw two dice. Add the numbers together.

Color in a box in the row above that number.

Soon you will build a wall.

What does your wall look like?

Can a mouse walk through your wall?

Look at a friend's wall. Does it look like your wall?

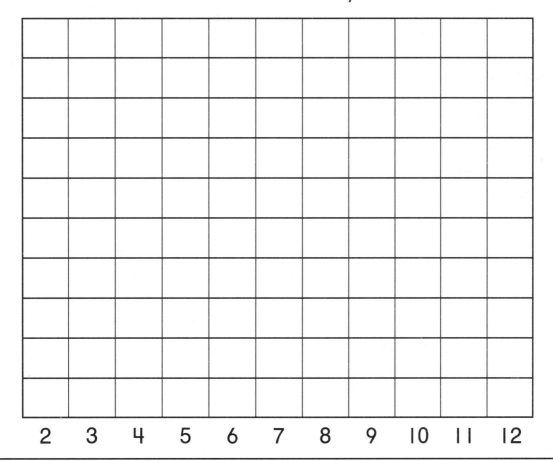

2	3	4	5	6	7	8	9	10	11	12

(Supports Big Book: *The Most Wonderful One of All*) **Constructing a bar graph.** To play this solo math game, each student needs a pair of dice. Read the game directions together. Demonstrate how to throw the dice, count up the dots, and enter the information on the graph. After students have played for a certain amount of time, have everyone stop and compare their "walls." Discuss the questions above the graph. Students can then continue playing the game and building their wall.

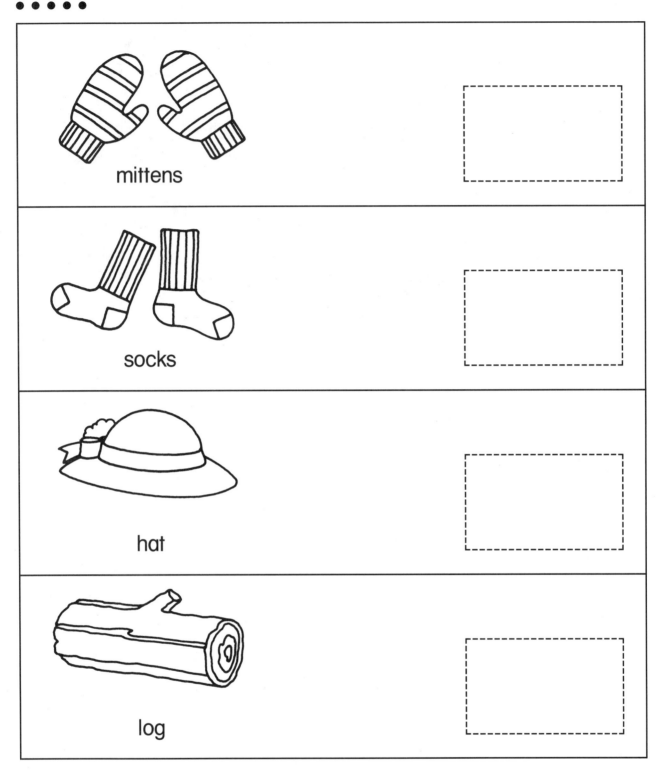

mittens

socks

hat

log

kittens

clocks

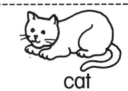

cat

frog

(Supports Student Book A, page 78) **Identifying rhyming words.** Students read each word on the left, then select a rhyming word from the word boxes at the bottom of the page. Students cut out and paste the word boxes in the correct places.

Home-School Connection

Sun Tea

You need:

2 herbal tea bags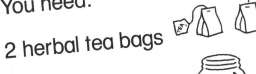

a large clear jar

ice

sugar or honey

the sun

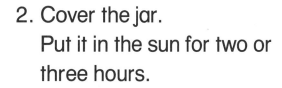

1. Fill the jar with cold water. Add two herbal tea bags.

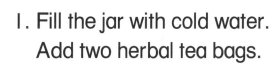

2. Cover the jar. Put it in the sun for two or three hours.

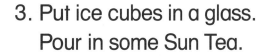

3. Put ice cubes in a glass. Pour in some Sun Tea.

4. Add sugar or honey, if you wish.

(Supports Student Book A, page 79) **Home-School Connection.** If possible, bring ingredients to school so students can make this recipe together. Then send the recipe home for students to enjoy with their families.

Cut the Word Bank cards from pages 98, 100 and 101.

Choose nine cards to glue on this game board.

Then play a game of Amazing Words tic tac-toe.

Key vocabulary reinforcement. Students prepare their game boards, then play a variation of tic-tac-toe with a partner. Each player has a different set of markers (paper clips, small pieces of colored paper, etc.) In order to place a marker on a square, a player must name the picture. The first player to place three markers in a row (horizontal, vertical, diagonal) wins the game. Save extra Word Bank cards for future use.